One Minute
PRAYERS
To Fuel Your Soul

STACY Y. WHYTE

Victorious Creations

Copyright © 2019 Stacy Y. Whyte

All rights reserved. No part of this book may be reproduced, distributed or transmitted in any form by any means, graphics, electronics, or mechanical, including photocopy, recording, taping, or by any means or stored in a database or retrieval system, written the prior written permission of the publisher except in the case of reprints in the context of reviews, quotes or references.

All bible scriptures reference taken from the Holy Writings in New King James Version, King James Version, New International Version and New Living Translation. Used by permission. All rights received. Printed in the United States of America.

First Edition: January 2019

"This is the confidence we have in approaching God: that if we ask anything according to his will, he hears us. And if we know that he hears us—whatever we ask—we know that we have what we asked of him."

1 John 15:14-15

Dedication

Dedicated to all the new believers that accepted Jesus Christ as their personal Savior and Lord of their soul and life.

Introduction

One Minute Prayers To Fuel Your Soul is an inspiration of the Holy Spirit. Though small in size it will help the new and seasoned believer to develop a consistent and constant prayer life before God.

Prayer is the key to gaining access to heaven and when it is not done on a regular basis the soil of your heart becomes dry because it is not being nourished and fueled by the Holy Spirit and Jesus Christ. The more you spend time with God, the more revelation, wisdom and knowledge He pours into you.

The prayers of a believer burn like blazing fire in the enemy's camp and destroys the work of the kingdom of darkness against you, your family, marriage, finances, health, ministry, business and career. The enemy is not laid back when it comes to preying on the children of God and you cannot be so busy that you forget to pray to God for divine protection, provision and elevation.

A life without prayer and direct communication with God is a direct injustice to yourself and those you love. God's heart towards you is gracious and compassionate, slow to anger and abounding in love and He wants you saved at all cost.

I originally did not intend to publish this, but I was encouraged by others to do so because they benefited from committing to the fifty-five days. It transformed their prayer life; now, they can go for thirty minutes to an hour in prayer. It is my hope that this little book will ignite something in you to start praying more and not wait until you have a challenging situation on hand. God is waiting to hear from you, all you need to do is show up before Him and the Holy Spirit will guide you—do not delay this is a clarion call for you to act now.

Day 1

Prayer For Today:

Gracious Father thank you for a sufficiency of self-confidence to rise up in faith to leap over the mountain of objections and injustice. Father give me the strength and resolve in my heart to triumph over fear and procrastination and help me to embrace the ladder of unshakeable faith. Father I know the plans you have for my life is prosper me and so I thank you for revealing your truth to me and leading me to fulfill my God given purpose in Jesus name, Amen.

Meditation Verse:

❀ *Hebrews 4:16* ❀

Day 2

Prayer For Today:

Gracious Father I uproot and renounce the spirit of rejection, abandonment, instability, anxiety, anger and double-mindedness from my life. Today I declare and decree that I am completely separated from them. I thank you for a renewed hope and faith. You have been my pillar of strength, the One that keeps me standing firm in everything that I do. Father help me to keep your words grounded in my heart so, that my daily practices will not go against your commands, statues and divine will in Jesus name, Amen.

Meditation Verse:

❈ ***Romans 12:2*** ❈

Day 3

Prayer For Today:

Heavenly Father thank you for healing me and setting me free from sickness, disease and affliction. Father I renounce all negative diagnosis and reports. I know you can do all things-you have healed the blind, the leper, the lame and even raised the dead. I stand on your promise that healing is the children's bread, I believe in your written word. Today, I declare that I am healed, delivered and set free from all sickness in Jesus name, Amen.

Meditation Verses:

❊ *Isaiah 53:4-5* ❊
❊ *Jeremiah 30:17-18* ❊

Day 4

Prayer For Today:

Gracious Father today I present my marriage to you, I ask you to sanctify my spouse and I, knit us closer together, renew our minds and love for each other daily. Teach us how to communicate with mutual respect by honoring each other. Father marriage is your institution help us to live in unity, in prayer and in love. Give us fresh love for each other and help us to keep you as the head of our union in Jesus name, Amen.

Meditation Verses:

❀ *Ecclesiastes 4:12* ❀
❀ *1 Peter 3:7* ❀
❀ *Proverbs 18:22* ❀

Day 5

Prayer For Today:

Sovereign Father I glorify your holy name; thank you for depositing your peace that surpasses all human understanding over me. I ask you to let your peace rest at the door that I walk in today. Help me to stand any test that may come my way without getting anxious, doubtful and fearful. I apply the Blood of Jesus Christ over my agenda for this day. I declare that I am the head and not the tail, I am above and not beneath, I rise above the enemy's plans and I will receive the results needed in Jesus name, Amen.

Meditation Verse:

❈ *Philippians 4:6-7* ❈

Day 6

Prayer For Today:

Holy and faithful are you Father; thank you for preparing me and equipping me to work diligently on the assignments that will come my way, open new doors of opportunities to me and bless me with a good position that will enable me to advance and excel. Father promotion does not come not from the east nor the west but it comes from you. God you know my capabilities, skills and talents, I thank you for the elevation that lies ahead for my financial and career advancement in Jesus name, Amen.

Meditation Verse:

❀ *Psalm 138:8*

Day 7

Prayer For Today:

Oh Father, Creator of the heaven and earth you are filled with all wisdom and knowledge. Thank you for giving me the insight on how to create and attract wealth in my life and how to sow back into the kingdom and others as I get promoted by you. Father I thank you for watching over my finances, my assets, my investments and for covering my seeds that are planted in the ground. Father just as you blessed Isaac a hundred-fold, I thank you for giving me a hundred-fold return on everything that I sow and plant in Jesus name, Amen.

Meditation Verse:

Luke 6:38

Day 8

Prayer For Today:

Father I pray for my children today, please protect them from the wicked one who desires to have their souls and rob them of their destiny. Father keep my children and their friends covered with the Blood of the Lamb and order their steps. Refresh their mind with your truth, breathe upon their gifts with your anointing, open the windows of heaven over them and release scholarships to them for college so they can honor you in their education and career in Jesus name, Amen.

Meditation Verse:

Psalm 127:3

Day 9

Prayer For Today:

Wonderful Father I break the yoke of depression, loneliness, oppression, panic attacks, heaviness, emotional and mental distress, obsessive compulsive behaviors and double-mindedness that causes my heart to be divided in commitment towards you. I renounce every negativity from my heart, my mind and my life and I declare that failure and defeat have no power over my life anymore. Today I thank you for my freedom, peace and joy of heart in Jesus name, Amen.

Meditation Verse:

❀ *Psalm 40:1-3* ❀

Day 10

Prayer For Today:

Sovereign Father thank you for igniting my passion to build a successful organization. Father I apply my heart to understanding and I incline my ear to your wisdom, I know it is more precious than rubies, so I thank you for teaching me your ways and leading as the CEO of this organization. Father let your blessings flow over on it so that it can benefit generations now and, in the future, provide employment to others, help families, youths and the community in the mighty name of Jesus, Amen.

Meditation Verses:

❀ *Exodus 35:35* ❀
❀ *Deuteronomy 25:13-15* ❀
❀ *Psalm 112:1* ❀

Day 11

Prayer For Today:

Father in heaven today I uproot and renounce the spirit of lack, poverty, setback and generational curses of deficiency off my life and my blood line. Thank you, Father, for blessing me abundantly so that in all things at all times I will abound in every good work and prosper. Father you believed in me when no one else did, you haven given me the knowledge needed to create and achieve what I was told by others I could not do. I know with you all things are possible. Today I declare and decree a supernatural overflow in my life in Jesus name, Amen.

Meditation Verse:

❀ *Psalm 106:4-5* ❀

Day 12

Prayer For Today:

Great and righteous Father you are wise in all your ways. Father thank you for giving me a heart to care for those in need, those in distress and in destitute situations. Thank you for the resources you have placed in my life and for pouring into my creativity and giving me the strategies to aid the less privilege, the homeless, those incarcerated, the widows and the orphans. Father give me the grace and strength to not grow weary in well doing but to press forward in Jesus name, Amen.

Meditation Verses:

❀ *Hebrews 6:10* ❀

❀ *Proverbs 19:17* ❀

Day 13

Prayer For Today:

Righteous Father thank you for giving me the grace to support others in their business and career adventures. As iron sharpens iron, I ask you Father to release your Holy Spirit upon me to saturate me in your wisdom and fill my mouth with your words to impart to others. Father thank you for using my mouth as an oracle to declare greatness over others and encourage them to push beyond the odds to stand in the position you desire for them to be, to lead and to grow in Jesus name, Amen.

Meditation Verse:

❀ *Philemon 1:7* ❀

Day 14

Prayer For Today:

Heavenly Father thank you for always guiding me, satisfying all needs and strengthening my frame. You chose me and predestined me to receive your unprecedented favor. You have been so faithful in covering me with your grace, I do not take it for granted but is very thankful. The anointing that you have placed on the gifts you have given me is opening doors to me that would ordinarily not be. Father thank you for allowing me to walk among great people in this world: locally, nationally and globally. I am humbled and grateful for the pureness of your love towards me Father in Jesus name I pray, Amen.

Meditation Verse:

❁ ***Proverbs 18:16*** ❁

One Minute Prayers

Day 15

Prayer For Today:

Wonderful Father this is a brand-new day with no condemnation, no guilt, no shame and no judgment; just a day of newness. Thank you, Father, for allowing your words to penetrate my heart and heal the wounds that are open. Father let your love and faithfulness never leave me, bind them around my neck and write them on the tablets of my heart so that I walk upright before you with my gifts as the doors gets opened for them to be used. Thank you for anointing my gifts and talents; help me to do everything with a spirit of excellence in Jesus name, Amen.

Meditation Verse:

❀ *Psalm 147:3-6* ❀

Day 16

Prayer For Today:

Heavenly Father I rise and shine to bring you glory in what I do today. I release the fire of the Holy Spirit against every spirit of witchcraft, Voodoo, Santeria and all evil powers and forces that the agents of darkness utilize against the purpose and destiny of the children of God. I cover my purpose and destiny with the blood of Jesus Christ. Thank you for your words of truth and deliverance today. Father help me to attain the goals that are set before me in this season in Jesus name, Amen.

Meditation Verse:

❀ Mark 16:17-18 ❀

Day 17

Prayer For Today:

Father I pray over my place of employment today. I surrender everything I do to you, as I work with my whole heart unto you and not others even though I honor those who lead in authority. I ask you to touch minds, regulate hearts and renew everyone's strength. Give us a spirit of excellence to serve our employer with joy and Father thank you for increase and promotion in my life and increase in the company's gross income so that all the employees can reap bountifully from its increase in Jesus name, Amen.

Meditation Verse

❀ *Psalm 75:6-7* ❀

Day 18

Prayer For Today:

Heavenly Father thank you for the opportunity to serve in your kingdom. Father help me to be steadfast, immovable, always abounding in your work, knowing that my labor before you is not in vain. I am your workmanship that was created for your good works, I trust your wisdom and guidance. I thank you for the Holy Spirit that constantly locates me and give me instructions with every new idea you have imprinted on the tablets of my heart. I know you will cause them to prosper and I praise you for it in advance in Jesus name I pray, Amen.

Meditation Verse:

❀ *Proverbs 4:5-9* ❀

Day 19

Prayer For Today:

Wonderful Father the godly insights you have graced me with is the cornerstone behind the success of my career. Thank you, Father, for continually revealing the secret treasures and the plans that you have set over my life from the foundations of the earth. Father thank you for the Holy Spirit that intercedes for my good and destroys the evil schemes of the enemy against my life and my family in Jesus name I pray, Amen.

Meditation Verse:

❈ *Proverbs 3:13-18* ❈

Day 20

Prayer For Today:

Father thank you for the revelation power of the Holy Spirit that is guiding my purpose and giving me a new blueprint for the enhancement, expansion and development of this wonderful business and career you've given me. Enlarge my territory, and allow Your hand to sustain me O God, keep me from harm so that I do not suffer unnecessarily. Father my life is an open book before you and my plans are not hidden from your sight bring me a victorious outcome and I will honor you in my giving in the name of Jesus, Amen.

Meditation Verse:

❈ *John 16:13* ❈

Day 21

Prayer For Today:

Thank you, heavenly Father, for helping my business to flourish and grow into a significant company within the community. Thank you for the connections and partners you have placed in my life. Father I ask you to keep the peace among us and help us to respect each other in our communication and not hold on to grudges but walk in forgiveness and love. O God help me to radiate your light before others, so that they may see your attributes in my good works and give you glory in Jesus name, Amen.

Meditation Verse:

❁ *Romans 15:5-6* ❁

Day 22

Prayer For Today:

Wonderful Father I renounce every negative voice mind binding spirit. I thank you for the destiny connectors that you are aligning with me and for the angelic gatekeepers that are watching over my destiny in this season. Thank you for creating opportunities, new contracts, grants and all types of resources for my career and business to thrive. Father help me to be a reflection of your Son in the corporate world and the nation in the name of Jesus, Amen.

Meditation Verse:

❁ *1 Corinthians 2:7-9* ❁

Day 23

Prayer For Today:

Wonderful Father I commit all that I am and will be to you. I ask you for guidance to overcome temptations as a single person, to rise above setbacks and to shape my life to be the way you intended from the foundations of the earth. Father I break every soul tie from the past and ask you to repair those fragmented pieces of my heart and soul so, that I can be whole. O Father, I trust you with my life and I know you'll take care of everything that concerns me and my future. I say goodbye to all of yesterday's disappointments and let downs, I welcome today with expectancy and anticipate my future of love and abundance in Jesus name, Amen.

Meditation Verse:

❀ ***James 1:12-15*** ❀

Day 24

Prayer For Today:

Righteous Father thank you for covering my investments from financial bandits, stock market crashes, financial mishandling and thieves. Father your word says, the plans of the diligent leads to profit and not loss and when we are faithful, we will abound in your blessings. Father touch my Financial Advisors heart, so they remain honest with my investments. I pray that you will bless this venture and help me to keep it saturated in prayer with integrity and zeal. Father I will tithe faithfully has you bring me increase to advance your work in Jesus name, Amen.

Meditation Verse:

❀ *Ecclesiastes 11:1-2* ❀

Day 25

Prayer For Today:

Father thank you for sharpening my leadership skills and abilities and for providing me with the tools needed to grow. Holy Spirit help me to lead with a heart of integrity and to not do anything from selfishness or empty conceit, but with humility of mind regarding others as more important than myself. Father strengthen your will in my life and lift up your countenance on the things that I have envisioned so I can break cultural, racial and economical barriers in Jesus mighty name, Amen.

Meditation Verse:

❀ *Numbers 6:24-26*

Day 26

Prayer For Today:

Heavenly Father I come against the spirit of pride, prejudice, arrogance, materialism, profane speech, jealousy and being critical of myself and others. Father help me to walk in humility with a compassionate heart for others. You have entrusted me with your favor and granted me the opportunity to be a steward over others, my finances and all the earthly gifts you have given me. Thank you for every good thing that you have placed in my life in Jesus mighty name, Amen.

Meditation Verse:

❁ *Proverbs 8:13-14* ❁

Day 27

Prayer For Today:

Father I choose to seek you first in all I do. My heart is always panting after you and I want to please you in every way. Father I ask you on this day to break every covenant and agreements that I am involved in that that you did not ordained and give me insight to connect with the right businesses, vendors, affiliates, customers and advertisers so that my company and career can flourish in such a competitive industry in Jesus name, Amen.

Meditation Verse:

❂ *Matthew 6:33-34* ❂

Day 28

Prayer For Today:

Father thank you for anointing my hands and my abilities to stand in greatness. Lord Jesus your precious blood continually cover the ideas and it causes them to bear fruits in the lives of those that cross my path. I am grateful to you Father for you who began a good work in me will continue to perfect it in Jesus name I pray, Amen.

Meditation Verse:

Psalm 90:17

Day 29

Prayer For Today:

Gracious Father I renounce every marine spirit that has and is trying to attach themselves to me. I disconnect myself from every familiar spirit, spiritual husband or spiritual wife that has connected to me through dreams and every other medium. I break these yokes from off of my life by the power of the Holy Spirit. Father I thank you for scattering, uprooting and destroying every devouring spirit away from my finances and binding up limitations and stagnation from off my life, business and career. Thank you, Father, for my liberation and for granting me serenity, joy and abundance in the name of Jesus, Amen.

Meditation Verse:

❀ *Malachi 3:11* ❀

Day 30

Prayer For Today:

Father please forgive me for the mistakes I have made that has caused hurt to myself and others. Deliver me from self-hatred and hatred for those who hurt me; deliver me from unforgiveness, bitterness of heart, sadness, resentment and malice towards others. Give me inner joy and a heart of love and forgiveness for all people. Father you are my hiding place, protect me from trouble and surround me with songs of deliverance and I will forever rejoice before you in Jesus name, Amen.

Meditation Verses:

❈ *Mark 11:22-26* ❈
❈ *Matthew 18:21-22* ❈

Day 31

Prayer For Today:

Father in heaven I present my children school, faculty and staff, coaches and bus drivers before you. I ask you to stretch out your hand over each of them, give them an expansion of compassion, knowledge and wisdom. Father give your angels charge over them to break negative cycles in their lives and fill them with your love for the students and their colleagues. I declare that no weapon formed against them will prosper in their life and the life of the students. Breathe upon these students and give them a renewed mind to focus and learn in Jesus name, Amen.

Meditation Verse:

Psalm 91:9-12

Day 32

Prayer For Today:

Father today I present the leaders of my nation to you and all governmental offices and officers to you. Holy Spirit I petition you with supplication and thanksgiving for all the leaders and all those in authority today I ask you to break yokes off their lives. Father deliver them from the spirit of pride and arrogance. Father give them humility and love for the people they govern over, help them to serve with integrity and seek you for wisdom. Keep corruption away from their heart and heighten their discernment in Jesus name, Amen.

Meditation Verse:
1 Timothy 2:1-4

Day 33

Prayer For Today:

Wonderful Father thank you for placing your hand upon me and anointing my head with fresh oil each new day. O God help me to guard what you have committed to my trust, avoiding useless, profane and idle babblings. Father direct me on how to correctly handle the word of truth and to watch over the souls of those in my care. Thank you for pouring into my spiritual gifts and sharpening them. So, I can flow freely in the five-fold ministry you have given me. Father increase my discernment, appoint the angels of healing, deliverance and breakthrough to me so, others can receive their deliverance through this ministry in Jesus name, Amen.

Meditation Verse:

1 Chronicles 4:9-10

Day 34

Prayer For Today:

Righteous Father today I pray for those who are suffering from abuse: domestic, sexual, financial, verbal and emotional abuse. Father deliver them and heal their pain. You took me out of the dark place of abuse, pain and addiction; you have crowned me with grace, compassion and love and I know you will do it for today's victims as well. Father you did not judge my past but you forgave me and turned my life of mess to a message that's now helping others to get up and get out. Father help me to articulate what needs to be said with fervor, compassion and love and guard me from the spirit of false pride and vain glory in Jesus name, Amen.

Meditation Verse:

❈ *Isaiah 35:10* ❈

Day 35

Prayer For Today:

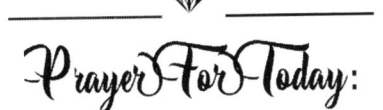

Glorious Father you are a wonderful God of love, mercy, favor and grace. Thank you for taking away insecurity, shame and disgrace of the past from me and planting seeds of favor in my life. As Esther found favor in your sight and David, I pray today that I will be favored by you and be found favorable in the eyes of people. Father as your beloved when I knock on a door, I declare it will be opened to me and when I ask for anything according to your will, I will receive it and wherever I go people will be attracted to sowing into my vision and ministry in Jesus name, Amen.

Meditation Verse:

❈ *Haggai 2:9* ❈

Day 36

Prayer For Today:

Father of heaven and earth, today I ask you to bind up the forces of darkness that is at work against your children. Father I bind up the spirit of suicide and murder. I shut up the first and second heaven and seal it up with the Blood of the Lamb. I annihilate the enemy and assassinate the wicked schemes of the agents of darkness against my life, my health, my ministry, my family and my finances. I declare victory, I am completely liberated in Jesus name, Amen.

Meditation Verse:

❀ Ephesians 6:12-16 ❀

Day 38

Prayer For Today:

Heavenly Father grant me the grace and clarity to fulfill the great commission you have placed on my life. Father help me to focus on the vision that is in front of me and show me how to effect change in lives that are broken and shattered from rape, abuse, dysfunctional backgrounds and addictions. Father I thank you for renewing the minds of those that are broken and igniting their faith to take leaps to receive the victory you have waiting ahead for them in Jesus name, Amen.

Meditation Verse:

❀ *Corinthians 1:3-5* ❀

Day 39

Prayer For Today:

Heavenly Father thank you for surrounding me with abundance, joy, love and strength. You are my strong tower and my helper. Father today I renounce shame and guilt from my life through the power of the Holy Spirit. Thank you for giving me heavenly access to soar and advance in the kingdom to bring honor to your name and win forgotten and lost souls through evangelism and outreach. Father I will run this race well for your glory in Jesus name, Amen.

Meditation Verses:

❀ *2 Timothy 2:15* ❀

❀ *Hebrews 12:1-3* ❀

Day 40

Prayer For Today:

Father I lift up my Doctors, Attorneys, Spiritual Advisors, Financial Counselors and Accountant before you. Father touch them today and pour into them from your reservoir of wisdom, renew the spirit of their mind for the tough decisions and choices they have to make for themselves and their clients. Give them a heart of flesh to serve with kindness and diligence and give them a spiritual ear to hear your voice and eyes to see what needs to be seen to benefit them, myself and other clients in Jesus name, Amen.

Meditation Verse:

❀ *Deuteronomy 8:18* ❀

Day 41

Prayer For Today:

Gracious Father thank you for crippling up and neutralizing every plan of the enemy against my health, my finances, my marriage, my children, my parents, my friendships and my business relationships. Father create in me a clean heart and renew a right spirit in me continually; so, I will not sin against you and others in my thoughts. Thank you for giving me the determination to push forward and produce overflow in every area of my life in Jesus name, Amen.

Meditation Verse:

❊ *Proverbs 16:7* ❊

Day 42

Prayer For Today:

Wonderful Father thank you for leading me in the path of goodness for your name sake. Father help me to resist every form of temptation of compromise. Every mind binding spirit that is trying to cause a battlefield in my mind I step on you now and release the fire of the Holy Spirit upon you. I am a child of the King of Kings and you cannot torment me and hinder my progress. I declare my mind is free and I am free in Jesus name, Amen.

Meditation Verse:

1 Corinthians 10:13

Day 43

Prayer For Today:

Heavenly Father use me as an instrument to unleash the strategic abilities you have anointed me with to the universe and let them be impactful to lives. Give me the inspiration to turn my thoughts into measurable goals that can bring increase to my ministry, business and career. You are the One who laid the foundations of the earth, so I know you own my beginning, my middle and my ending. Father set my feet back on the path you designed just me to thread on and keep me grounded and committed to what you set before me to do in Jesus name, Amen.

Meditation Verse:

❈ *Proverbs 3:5-6* ❈

Day 44

Prayer For Today:

Righteous Father bless this day and grant me a day that stretches beyond every limitation, difficulties, setbacks and challenges. Father let the heavens open over me and the showers of your blessings from your treasury flow down on me. Holy Spirit you are my comforter, I welcome you into my day. Order my steps and allow me to experience joy, your supernatural abundance and growth as I move forward in the plans you have for my life in Jesus name, Amen.

Meditation Verse:

❀ *John 14:26* ❀

Day 45

Prayer For Today:

Heavenly Father thank you for touching every financial transaction that I am doing in season. Thank you for removing all negative information that may be posted on my credit report and releasing to me the credit score that I need to attain the approval that I am seeking. I declare that my credit score is now perfect. Father thank you for bringing increase to my life and my ministry through these transactions in Jesus name, Amen.

Meditation Verse:

Deuteronomy 28:12

Day 46

Prayer For Today:

Gracious Father I present the youths in my church, community and nation before you. I come against the spirit of bullying, peer pressure, bad association, depression, sexual immorality and secret societies that lures the youths into blood rituals and other ungodly acts that are against the will of God. I declare that the youths are growing into honorable men and women that will glorify God in prayer, worship and spending time in the word to grow spiritually and in their life in Jesus name, Amen.

Meditation Verse:

✤ Proverbs 25:21-22 ✤

Day 47

Prayer For Today:

Righteous Father I ask you to supernaturally cancel any debt that has become a burden in my life and my family's life. Restore the peace we had before all these debts, that are knocking at our door and help us to manage our finances to glorify you. Teach us how to budget and live within our means and be faithful tithers in your kingdom. As you restore me, show me the ministries and organizations to sow in and make it prosper in Jesus name, Amen.

Meditation Verse:

❀ *Romans 13:8* ❀

Day 48

Prayer For Today:

Holy Father in heaven grant me the audacious courage to conquer the things that are not of you: fear, doubt, unbelief, smoking, drug-sex-alcohol addictions, lying, idolatry, stealing, adultery, pornography and everything else that brings reproach to your name and stagnation to my career, my marriage, my finances, my ministry and my business. Exalt me O Lord to a higher level of commitment to you and grant me good success in Jesus name, Amen.

Meditation Verse:

Ephesians 1:18

Titus 2:11-12

Day 49

Prayer For Today:

Heavenly Father thank you for blessing the work of hands and causing whatever I touch to blossom into a dynasty of empowerment, encouragement, hope, advancement, enlightenment and success for the youth's lives to be built up, enhanced and transformed into the men and women God desires for them to be in Jesus name, Amen.

Meditation Verse:

Jeremiah 17:8

Day 50

Prayer For Today

Father today I lift up my spiritual leaders before you. I ask you Father to strengthen them, help them to live in righteousness and holiness and reflect the love of Christ for your people. Provide for them and keep them, bless their bread and water, keep sickness and disease away from them, give them revelation knowledge to impart to your people and everywhere their feet thread cause them to diffuse the fragrance of the Gospel of peace to others in Jesus name, Amen.

Meditation Verse:

1 Thessalonians 5:12-13

Day 51

Prayer For Today:

Sovereign God I come before you today for my nation. I ask you to put a edge of protection around us, cover us from disasters, terrorist attacks, economic meltdown, witchcraft, lawlessness, apostasy and the infiltration of evil powers and acts that causes premature death. Help us to pray without ceasing and to live at peace with each other in Jesus name, Amen.

Meditation Verse:

2 Chronicles 7:14

Day 52

Prayer For Today:

Father thank you for the vision, mandate and the mantle you have placed over my life. Thank you for making me adequate and equipping me for every good work and for granting me my heart's desire to accomplish great milestones and leap over the valley of challenges to embark upon the mountain of success that is creating a legacy for the generation to come. in Jesus name, Amen.

Meditation Verse:

❈ *Proverbs 13:22* ❈

Day 53

Prayer For Today:

Father I present my parents before you; I ask you to grant them extension of days with good health, provision, strength and inner joy. Help them to live a life that is pleasing in your sight and cause their latter to be greater Father. Speak your words of revelation, inspiration and wisdom to them so they can encourage the younger generation to press beyond the challenges and disappointments of life as they did in Jesus name, Amen.

Meditation Verse:

Lamentations 3:22-23

Day 54

Prayer For Today:

Wonderful Father I renounce the spirit of church hurt, betrayal, broken promises and all unfulfilled vows in marriage, relationships, business and ministry, that may have caused hurt to myself and others. I ask you to release me from all guilt that I may carry in my heart because of what I previously did. Father I thank you for releasing me from unfruitful relationships that entangle me into temptation and sin. Father I thank you that today the curse of miscarriage and unfruitfulness of my vision and purpose is over in Jesus name, Amen.

Meditation Verse:

Jeremiah 29:11

Day 55

Prayer For Today:

Father of heaven and earth thank you for bringing complete restoration to me. Father for all the things that the enemy has stolen from me, I declare a seven-fold restitution over my life. Thank you for your deliverance power and for choosing me to serve my generation. Above all, thank you for equipping me with the skills and resources needed to be effective and efficient so, I can bring you glory in Jesus name, Amen.

Meditation Verse:

Joel 2:25-26

Epilogue

The number 55 represents

Grace Upon Grace

We are in the dispensation of God's grace but that grace should never be taken for granted, be abused, manipulated or seen as an excuse to sin. While grace is extended to you, a life without true repentance is only an empty shell that becomes bankrupt in heavenly places.

Repentance comes with the act of prayer, acknowledging that a wrong was done and being truly sorry within your heart for that act. Repentance means you let it go to God, you stop the sin and do not return to it. Subsequently, you don't hold unto the guilt and shame that often accompanies the sin that was committed.

After repentance you are washed in the precious Blood of the Lamb all

Stacy Y. Whyte

you need to do is walk in accordance with God's statures, commands and decrees and He will work everything else out for you, so that, you can live righteously and abundantly for His glory.

"Peter said to them, "Each one of you must turn away from your sins and be baptized in the name of Jesus Christ, so that your sins will be forgiven; and you will receive God's gift, the Holy Spirit." – Acts 2:38

"If you openly declare that Jesus is Lord and believe in your heart that God raised him from the dead, you will be saved. For it is by believing in your heart that you are made right with God, and it is by openly declaring your faith that you are saved." – Romans 10:9-10 NLT

Salvation Prayer

Lord Jesus today I humble myself
before you. I know that
you died for me so that I can inherit
eternal life. Lord
I repent of my sins and I ask you to
wash me in your precious blood
and receive me in the kingdom of
God today in Jesus name I pray,
Amen.

Stacy Y. Whyte

Other Books by the Author

All books available on Amazon and Barnes & Noble, iTunes and Nook.

Connect with the Author:
WWW.YOURFAITHFACTOR.COM

Made in the USA
San Bernardino, CA
10 March 2019